C000066674

Loving you is easy – Loving me is hard!

Developing healthy self-esteem and confidence

Libby Hammond

Published by Birkhall Media
ISBN: 978-1-907146-20-6

DEDICATION

To Dick, Natalie, Tom, Poppy and Jules and to Peter – loving you is always easy!

Loving you is easy – Loving me is hard!

Acknowledgements

Many thanks to Dick for editing, Peter for helping with the title, Angie Taylor for prompting me to put all this on paper, and Anne Redpath with for her eye for detail. Gratitude to the very talented Shona Warwick and Tom Harmer who sorted the models and Robin Sieger and Roy Sheppard for their patient technical help. A huge thanks to Seth Gardner for taking chairs to the beach to create a beautiful book cover. Finally many thanks to Kim and Eric Rowlands and Philip and Dee Allen for sharing this journey.

CONTENTS

Loving you is easy – Loving me is hard!

Introduction

It was one of those moments when I wanted the ground to open up and swallow me. I'd memorised the poem for the class presentation, had gone over it for several days (well actually mostly the night before and while munching cereal and toast that morning!), I had launched into the first couple of lines, but then became conscious of everyone looking at me, and my mind went blank! Tension was holding hands with the silence that filled the room. I frantically tried to remember what came next, then started to feel...what was I feeling?..very embarrassed. Apart from remembering that awful feeling, the other thing I remembered was the teacher telling me something along the lines of 'sit down and we'll move onto ...'. Interestingly, in the following years, whenever something went wrong in what I was doing, that feeling of being *passed over* would be a recurring theme.

Now before you read any further, it may be that you have an interest in spiritual things. You may have a committed faith, or no views one way or another. What I'd like to say is that the models and principles in this book have really worked in helping individuals flourish in confidence and self-respect so please take out the things that are of most help to you and leave the bits that aren't!

I'd like to ask you a few questions: have you ever had experiences where something has gone wrong that has left you feeling less good about yourself and you've had trouble completely shaking the negative thoughts off because they follow a recurring theme? Do you have moments when you feel you don't measure up to your own expectations - never mind those of other people? Are you longing to have an intimate relationship with God but have a secret suspicion that, with all your failings, you aren't really 'good enough' to register on His radar? If so, that is fantastic as this book is for you \o/

Let me explain.

I had headed off to hang up washing one sunny summer's day and a question kept going through my head – what is the abundant life? I had been reading John 10:10 *'The thief comes only to steal and kill and destroy; I came that they may have life and have it abundantly'* (ESV). The New Living Translation says *'...to give them a rich and satisfying life'*. From

5

what I'd seen, an 'abundant' or 'satisfying' life seemed to be a mixture of what level of possessions, health, successful job, marriage and children a person had compared to someone else. Spiritual 'success' often seemed to be measured in the same way; how big is our church, what 'position' do we have or how busy are we in church, what spiritual gifts do people recognise in my life, etc. Any feeling of 'lack' seemed to lead to a whole lot of 'dis's – discontentment, disheartened, dispirited, distrustful and disengaged to name but a few.

Communication isn't a meeting of words, it's a meeting of meaning, so as I hung up the washing, I began exploring with God what He meant by 'abundant life'.   I asked Him the question – what is the one thing of any real meaning that the thief can 'steal, kill and destroy'?

I had an epiphanal moment before the Lord!

It was as if the Lord spoke these words into my head and heart: 'Libby, the abundant life is when you really love being the person I have created you to be. I want you to know every aspect of who I have made you to be, warts and all. When you come to me and say, "Father, thank you for me, my personality, my character, the way I look and my soul- you Father are my sufficiency and my satisfaction," Libby, you have no idea how much joy that brings to my heart. Be aware of this: the only thing the enemy can attempt to steal that really matters is your standing as a daughter of the King of Kings. If he can rob you of your joy in who I have made you to be, it is not just you who is diminished, but it hurts my Father's heart. Don't give the enemy grounds for celebration.'   Wow!

This book is written so that you can understand and grow in who God has made you to be.   It will look at understanding what sabotages our confidence in who God has made us to be, and we will learn ways of dealing with that once and for all. We'll explore how to be the 'aroma of Christ' at work and at home by stepping into the fullness of who the Lord has made us to be – not as something we are working at but out of the overflow of what is already in our hearts. Each chapter will have useful activities, bible references, questions and ...some great stories and quotes. We'll also look at entering into 'garden time' with the Lord, even in the middle of a roomful of people, so that we stay mindfully focused on His presence with us every moment of our lives.

I have integrated John 10:10 into the material I use for business and education, and the models and activities have been used in the UK, USA, Canada and South Africa so I know it works! There is a great African proverb: *'When there is no enemy within, the enemy outside cannot hurt you.'*

My heart is to see you, no matter what age or stage you are at, really understand how you can make a stand against the robbery of who you are created to *'be'*, grow in spending time in the garden with God and take this awesome message into the lives of those around you. You were created for a purpose, and an essential part of stepping into that purpose is understanding that the Lord would say of you - *"loving you is easy"*. I really pray that as you go through this book, you will come to understand how important it is to know and learn to love yourself for who you are, decide to choose life for yourself, irrespective of how you *'feel'* about yourself or your circumstances, and........stay in the abundant life your Father in Heaven has prepared for you in His Presence.

Libby Hammond
Dumfries Hogmanay 2013
www.confidentcommunicators.uk.com

Chapter 1 – Going round in circles

I'd turned on the radio on New Year's Day while waiting for the kettle to boil and caught the lyrics of a song which went something like this: '*I'm just trying to work out how to be like myself, I'm just trying to work out these cards I've been dealt*'. It seems that some of the most common themes in films, songs, poetry etc run along the lines of "*Who am I? Where am I going?*"...or "*Someone come and find me as I need LOVE.*"

There is a story about a woman who went to her husband and asked him for the money for a face lift – she was sagging a little and felt a bit of help was needed to rescue her from further southward movement. Her husband, having heard it would cost a few thousand pounds, suggested she ask God, which she duly did. '*Lord, I could do with some improvements in the beauty department... I'm sagging!*', so the Lord said to go ahead and have the surgery. The results were amazing and she looked 20 years younger. Unfortunately, two months later she was knocked down and killed. She was furious as she stood before the Lord: '*I don't understand this, I asked you if I could go ahead and have surgery, you said yes, I go through it all, look amazing and the next thing is I'm dead*' To which the Lord replied, '*I didn't recognise you!*'

'*If it weren't for caffeine, I'd have no personality whatsoever!*' Anonymous

What is it that causes us to have challenges in loving who we have been made to be? Until we arrive in heaven, we will never really understand what it cost our Father in Heaven to send His son to die on the cross for us. Nor what it cost Jesus to go to the cross. What we do know is that His love for us is so great that Jesus went through with His Father's plan to bring us into relationship with Him. The sacrifice of the cross wasn't easy but loving us is. However, it seems that from the Lord's point of view, and our biggest challenge, is that we can love the Lord and other people but find it really hard to love ourselves. Hence the title of the book: Loving you is easy – Loving me is hard!

We tend to focus on what we fail in or lack, and the wrong things we do, say or think. It is the link between how we love who we have been made to be and the confidence that can bring, that is probably the greatest key to living the abundant life, and, bringing the Kingdom of Heaven into the lives of those around us.

Back to the beginning

The participants were all seated, ready to learn about how to give confident and effective presentations.

The first activity was really straightforward; all they needed to do was to find a partner, stand in a space in the room and then decide who would go first in talking. Number '1' had to talk for one minute on their favourite holiday while number '2' listened. Then this was to be repeated with number '2' talking and number '1' listening. All went to plan and there were lots of smiles and obvious enjoyment as people recounted great food, hilarious stories about confusing words in the local language, tales of airport waits and bargain flights.

Body language reinforced the relaxed talking with lots of smiling and movement, hands being used like paintbrushes to paint a picture of the sea, size of rooms and so on. When asked how they enjoyed talking, everyone said they found it a pretty relaxed and straightforward experience.

I then asked them to repeat the exercise except this time the subject they had to talk on for one minute was: *'What do you love about who you are as a person?'* I asked them to only use words that described their personality, character and talents – basically to give their partner a picture of who they *'be'*. Sounds of *'eek'*, *'aargh'* and somewhat shocked facial expressions were followed by a deafening silence when I started the one minute timer. A couple of people made it to one minute with the majority petering out within the first 30 seconds and comments ranged from 'how embarrassing', *'I can't think of anything'* to *'I've never really thought about that'*.

When I asked for feedback on how they felt when talking about themselves, common answers were *'embarrassed'*, *'sounds like I'm big-headed'*, concern about what the partner might be thinking eg ' *I think I'm funny but they might not'* or *'I can't think of anything'*. At the same time there were about 3% who enjoyed themselves and came out with a raft of descriptive words such as strategic, good organiser, kind, love my family, honest etc.

I've used this exercise internationally with all sorts of socio-economic groups in all sorts of sectors and the results are almost always the same. About 94-97% of any group of participants will say they don't feel confident in talking about who they be. The really sad thing is that this statistic is the same for those who have committed themselves to God as it is for people who haven't - they know they love God, they know God loves them but there is a little – or sometimes major – niggling thought that they aren't *good enough* for their Heavenly Father to really love them. The result can be one of two extremes; either giving up seeking to grow in intimacy with the Lord, or, becoming driven to earn His approval.

Either way we find our minds going round in negative conversational circles with ourselves, and that is when what I call the *'internal terrorists'* get a foot in the door, and make a very good job of sabotaging our confidence.

We'll come to the *'internal terrorists'* and where they come from in the next chapter. For the moment we need to understand the dynamics behind why at a personal level we find talking about ourselves a bit of a struggle. By understanding what is going on, it is so much easier to put solutions in place to deal with these 'terrorists' once and for all. And that's a joy!

<u>Working things out - the Cycle of Works</u>

CYCLE OF WORKS

The Cycle of Works is based on Dr Frank Lake, Clinical Psychologist's work

I'd like you to think of a time when you achieved something that made you feel really good. You might have a memory of being part of a winning team or getting a job because of a successful interview, a project that went really well or trying a new recipe everyone thought was delicious. Whatever the event, how would you rate the *'feel good'* factor you experienced? The answer might cover words like *'great'*, *'on top of the world'*, *'very satisfied'* etc. Success helps us feel good about ourselves and, isn't it good to be able to talk about our Achievements with our peer group – thinking of the round robin Christmas letters with fulsome information on amazing holidays, job moves, sporting prowess...etc!

The feelings that accompany success lead on to a sense of Significance - we feel good about ourselves and have a sense of self worth and of being valued. The impact of that *'feel good'* factor is that it creates a very positive, empowered and motivated mind-set otherwise known as Sustaining Strength or the *'buzz'*. In short, the kind of energy that gets you out of bed in the morning. After all, if that last souffle was such a success, there's no reason why that other recipe you've been waiting to try will be any less successful. It may be a new report you've to prepare or trying out a new golf club – whatever it is, yesterday's success is a strong motivator for expecting more success. It can be quite a heady emotional experience.

'That's the difference between me and the rest of the world! Happiness isn't good enough for me! I demand euphoria!' Calvin (Calvin and Hobbes)

Now we can look around our peer group, heads held high, with a strong sense of self and peer Acceptance based on what we have achieved. Is this not true?

Now the key question is: how do you like this model? *"Sounds good"* I hear you say, and it does seem like a very good model. Indeed it is the model that probably 97% of the population live by. However, it's not a healthy model – why? If you play a rubbish game of golf, don't get called for an interview, or the soufflé collapses just as it is about to be served, are you still feeling so good about yourself?

Self-doubt starts to raise its head and while we might be geared up to redoing the souffle, there may be a slight niggle of 'hope this works this time'. Self-doubt makes it harder for us to be quite so motivated and engaged with what we are involved with and, most importantly, we find it harder to feel accepted in our peer group and be happy with who we are. Thoughts fill our head: *'They must be laughing at me'*, *'Their souffle was spectacular'*, *'Their project got backing'*,...you will no doubt be able to think of something like this!

The little niggles of self-doubt tend to come through as negative words or thoughts about ourselves – I call these the *'internal terrorists'* – and we're going to look at how to deal with these in the next chapter!

The Cycle of Works is the cycle of who we *'do'*; we tend to describe ourselves by what we have achieved, our competencies, and our sense of self-value and acceptance is based primarily on what we've achieved.

The Dance of Disengagement

Interestingly most education systems globally tend to test pupils on the knowledge and skills they have gained in specific subjects. For pupils who have no talent for a particular subject, for example, numbers or language, lack of achievement and an inability to express how they feel about this, becomes a major source of frustration, disappointment and ultimately disengagement!

This sense of failure to achieve affects every aspect of life – whether it's the young mum feeling she can't cope with breast-feeding, the parish minister who struggles with chairing meetings or the Director of a company whose marriage is failing. This feeling of failure is particularly reinforced for those who have had abusive backgrounds.

Globally there are real challenges with people disengaging from work, young people disengaging from school – even as early as at nursery level, - unemployed people disengaging from hope. Many Christians are also driven by a desire to repay God for His free gift and so get caught up in a lot of good activities around the church – and then haven't the time to meet up with friends whose lives aren't faith-based! There is a saying that if the devil can't stop you being busy for Jesus, he'll jump on your back and work you to death. In the middle of all the *'doing'* of the Christian life there can be an inner gnawing dissonance. Our prayers are not being answered, we are facing really difficult life circumstances. It seems we have to wait a very long time for the Lord to lift us out of a difficult situation. All this can often confirm what we'd always suspected - despite all our 'commitment' we hear a little voice in our heads saying 'You're not even a very good Christian and your Heavenly Father thinks you're a failure'.

Pirates and Paintings

Do you remember the dream you had about what you wanted to be when you grew up? As a child, you probably created and played in an amazing imaginary world where you might be an astronaut helping discover new planets, or found a piece of cloth that transformed you into a superhero that saved the Lego people from a T Rex.

We became quite engrossed and very imaginative and passionate about our story. For parents, the latent talent that promised a great future for our children could be seen in its embryonic stages.

As we engaged with education our goals shifted from what now seems 'impractical' (who needs pirate captains these days!), towards 'employability' and 'income opportunities'. These require more than imaginative play. They require the acquisition of knowledge and skills. That's the reality of life isn't it?

Interestingly, if you ask pupils why they go to school, the most common answers are: 'We have to' or 'It's the law' or 'You need to go to school to get a job'. Very few young people see school as a means of helping them achieve their dream. In addition, for many young people, academic requirements (passing exams in subjects we have to do) don't always match up to their natural talents and strengths and this can create a lack of motivation and reinforce their sense of disengagement.

I am sure many of you reading this will remember painful sessions with for example mental arithmetic, or, in the art class when your picture of a vase and flowers was mistaken for an erupting volcano! Additionally, because in the Cycle of Works model, language is developed around who we 'do' rather than who we 'be', people can often have difficulty expressing how they feel. If we can't express how we feel we can go down various degrees of one of two routes: we either implode (withdraw) or explode (anger driven reactions). Either way we disengage, and negative labelling of failure by our peers can compound these results.

A 1999 Gallup Poll demonstrated that for any workforce in any country globally approximately 13% of the workforce were at work and were engaged, 67% were at work, and the rest never turned up. When what we 'do' fails or goes wrong we are more likely to disengage. Competent confidence will not sustain engagement or give us influence with those around us. Lack of success leading to disengagement with self is reflected in disengagement with people and life – at a personal, work and spiritual level.

GREAT NEWS – the Cycle of Grace

CYCLE OF GRACE

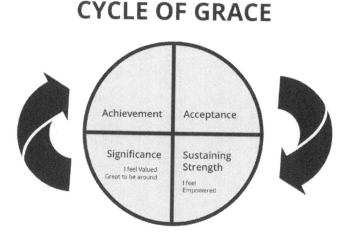

I love the Cycle of Grace, in fact I love grace. One of my favourite verses is John 1:16 'From His fulness have we received grace upon grace'.

This Cycle demonstrates beautifully how to develop authentic confidence – both in ourselves and especially in the Lord and who He has made us to be. The power and strength of this cycle is based on who we 'be', and where we can describe ourselves: our personality, talents, strengths, abilities and passion. When we Accept and really like ourselves for who we 'be' – focussing on strengths and recognising but not getting side-tracked into weaknesses - we will feel empowered and have a healthy self-esteem that won't fall to pieces when something we are 'doing' goes wrong. By developing descriptive language around who we are and by being able to express how we feel about things, 'failure' doesn't stop us from achieving our dreams. By being able to express how we feel we don't need to explode or implode (withdraw).

'I have not failed. I've just found 10,000 ways that won't work.' Thomas Edison

This approach makes it easier for us to see the relevance of learning knowledge and skills for areas in which we have natural talents and abilities. We can stay very engaged because we are able to hold onto our dream. As a result we will go on to achieve something that, for us, has a meaningful outcome – although that might not always meet other people's expectations! Remember the circumstances of your life do not diminish the value of who you 'be' and the good you can bring to those around you. The negative aspects of the past, with their associated memories, is for 'reference' but not for 'residence'. By residence I mean where we revisit a scenario and relive all the emotions associated with it rather than choosing to move on.

What is fantastic is that the Cycle of Grace means that when the Lord says He loves us unconditionally and we read John 10:27 'My sheep listen to my voice; I know them, and they follow me. I give them eternal life, and they shall never perish; no-one can snatch them out of my hand', our hearts can leap with confidence and joy knowing that this is true for you and me. 'But', I hear you say, 'I'm a rubbish sinner'.

This is true, but, because of the wonderful Cross, you are a glorious ruin, and one day you will be perfect. Anyway, what does Col 3:1-3 say? It says 'Since, then, you have been raised with Christ, set your hearts on things above, where Christ is seated at the right hand of God. Set your minds on things above, not on earthly things. For you died and your life is now *hidden with Christ in God'.* I can only say 'Woo Hoo'- fabulous.

Ogres and Onions

We've looked at how fantastic it is to know and understand who we be so here's a question for you. What is your passion in life (try to avoid being hyper analytical about this, I'm just looking for the first thing that pops into your head!)? You might say; music, football, wine, cooking, travel, people, the bible etc. Let's do a little exercise here – I call it the Onion model but my son Peter calls it the Shrek model because, yes you've got it, ogres are like onions!

On a sheet of paper, write down whatever your passion in life is. Now draw a large circle underneath the word. So here is the first question: why is that particular thing important to you? Write down your answer next to that outside circle.

Now draw a circle inside the larger one (in effect the next layer inside) and here is the second question: how does that make you feel? Once you write down the answer to that question we can draw the next onion layer inside that one and ask the question: why is that feeling important to you?

Your layers should look something like this:

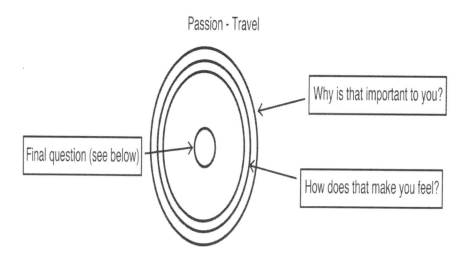

Passion - Travel

Why is that important to you?

Final question (see below)

How does that make you feel?

Continue asking yourself the same two questions (Why is that important to you? How does that make you feel?) until you have created about 6-8 layers in your onion. Now here is the final question: when you have spent time with people, (it could be a meal at friends, going out for an evening or a works night out), and they are leaving to go home, how do you like them to go away feeling about themselves?

Your answers might run something like this:

- Why is that important to you? - I like seeing new places
- How does seeing new places make you feel? - I feel free and engaged
- Why is being free and engaged important to you? - I am more motivated when I am in control of my life
- How does being in control of your life make you feel? - It makes me feel empowered
- Why is being empowered important to you? - I can get things done and don't get held back
- FINAL QUESTION: when people have left your company after spending time together, whether socially or at work, how do you like them to go away feeling about themselves? - I like them to go away feeling empowered and with a *'can-do'* attitude

Do you see how our core passion relates to who we *'be'* and our passion relates to how we *'do'*? The reality is that we carry our core passion into everything we do and wherever we go. We'll look at this again in Chapter 3 but for the moment, what is so important to understand is this – when we turn up somewhere for whatever reason be it work, home, social events or whatever, we take ourselves with us. If I know that my *'core passion/driver'* is to leave people with a *'can-do'* feeling, then by mindfully using that, I can have a hugely positive effect on those around me. Our core passion is the place from which we influence.

Reflective Exercises:

1 Write down at least 20 positive words that describe your personality, character, talents and abilities. (If you get stuck, think of what qualities you would look for in a friend and then ask yourself which of these words would apply to you – this usually helps a lot!)

2 Write down at least 5 of your spiritual strengths/gifts.

3 Ask a friend or some family to be your 'audience' and stand up and share, in one minute, all the words on both your lists from 1) and 2), starting by saying: 'My name is ...and I am amazing because...'

4 Write a list of at least 20 aspects of God's personality and character (it would be really useful to also write down relevant bible references and mark alongside them how you have personally experienced those particular aspects eg Psalm 86:5. 'You Lord, are forgiving and good, abounding in love to all who call to you'.

5 Choose two verses from the bible that really mean something to you about how God loves you. If you've never done it before, spend the next few days memorising and meditating on these verses. Read them at the start of the day, thank God for what they mean and that He wrote them for you to hold on to. Think about how the Lord has shown you the truth of these verses in the course of your day – His Presence is with you.

6 You might want to start a journal, especially to record where you see the Lord touching your life in little ways – even if it is thanking Him for a parking space!

Bible verses worth exploring:

1 Exodus 25:30 – 35. In what ways can you see the Lord developing and equipping individuals?

2 Deuteronomy 32:10. Can you think of times when the Lord has rescued you? What does it mean to know you are the apple of the Lord's eye? Apparently the *'apple of the eye'* is the most sensitive part of the eye.

3 Ps 139:1-16. Take one verse each day and think about what your Father in heaven is saying to you about you. You might like to journal what you discover.

4 Matthew 22:37, 38. If you really loved yourself (who the Lord has created you to be), how much easier would it be to love the Lord with all your heart, mind and soul, - and your neighbour? If you loved the Lord with all your heart, mind and soul, how much easier would it be to believe Him when He says you are loved by Him?

For reflection:

A great friend, Jolee Martinez, sent me this via email:

Psalm 23*

The Lord is my Shepherd..........that's Relationship!
I shall not want.........that's Supply!
He makes me lie down in green pastures.......that's Rest!
He leads me beside the still waters........that's Refreshment!
He restores my soul..........that's Healing!
He leads me in paths of righteousness..........that's Guidance!
For His name's sake.............that's Purpose!
Though I walk through the valley of the shadow of death..........that's Testing!
I will fear no evil.........that's Protection!
For You are with me.............that's Faithfulness!
Your rod and staff comfort me................that's Discipline!
You prepare a table before me in the presence of my enemies.......that's Hope!
You anoint my head with oil.............that's Consecration!
My cup runs over................ that's Abundance!
Surely goodness and mercy will follow me all the days of my life.........that's Blessing!
And I will dwell in the house of the Lord................that's Security!
Forever.......that's Eternity!

*http://www.appleseeds.org/Ps-23_Explained.htm

Chapter 2 – Sorting out the Internal Terrorists!

In Chapter 1 we looked at how motivating and empowering it is when we are able to really love who God has made us to 'be' rather than letting perceived failure dispirit and de-motivate us – and feed the 'internal terrorists'. In this chapter, I'd like to look at where the 'internal terrorists' come from and how we can deal with them. Result? Confidence in who God has made us to be, a renewed sense of trust in Him, a deeper assurance of His good purpose and plan for our lives.

The Lego approach

As people, we have five areas of personal functioning: spiritual, rational, volitional, physical and emotional (not in any order of importance!). These areas are influenced, developed, damaged, restored and healed over the years, starting from the day we are born. From the moment we arrive in the world, our little internal video-camera continues recording everything we experience.

We don't necessarily understand the context or circumstances of what is happening around us but we do register how we are feeling. As we grow up, we progress through 8 building block stages of emotional development which are nicely outlined by psychoanalyst Erik Erickson.

Life's circumstances and events cause cracks in the stack of building blocks which only become evident (and this can be years later) when we find ourselves under pressure.

Erickson's 8 Stages of Emotional Development

This is a great model to demonstrate the development of 'cracks'.

65 - death	Integrity (accept one's life) Vs Despair (no self satisfaction)
40-65 years	Compassion and parenting Vs Stagnation (no giving or learning)
19-40 years	Intimacy Vs Isolation (fear of committed relationship)
12-18 years	Identify (belief in Self) Vs Role Confusion
6-12 years	Industry (work) Vs Inferiority (what I do isn't good enough)
3-6 years	Initiative (independence) Vs Guilt (what I do is wrong)
1.5-3 years	Autonomy (self determination) Vs Doubt in self value
1-1.5 years	Trust Vs Mistrust (anxiety)

For example, a young mum with a two year old child has rushed home from the shops, laden with bags which need to be unpacked before she dashes out to pick up her 6 year old from school. She gets everything into the kitchen and realises she is going to be late when the two year old pipes up '*I need the toilet*', then a second later says '*Oops*' and a little puddle appears on the floor. The mother, hot and bothered from all the rushing about, loses her patience and in a frustrated tone of voice cries '*You stupid child, now we'll be late*' and proceeds to whip off the wet clothes, put on fresh ones and hurtles them both out the house. Now the mother loves her two year old – she is just under a lot of pressure and had '*let off steam*'.

By the time they pick up the 6 year old, chatted with other mums at the school gate about potty training followed by a post school run cup of coffee, all is sweetness and light. The 2 year old however, has video'd everything and internalised how he/she felt, without understanding the context. The mother wasn't saying her child was stupid - she was just stressed, - however, the feeling the child is left with might be shame or embarrassment. A crack develops in that particular building block stage which might affect emotional responses in subsequent years.

Whatever it was like for you as you were growing up, the truth is everyone has cracks in their building blocks – isn't that encouraging? You are not alone. The important thing to understand is that when our '*stack*' comes under pressure, the feeling associated with a particular crack become evident. Think of the last time you felt less good about yourself – whether at work, out with friends, with family or whatever. What word/s would describe how you felt? Now here's a question – hold the feeling and think of how old you feel. For example you might be 45 but at that moment you feel as if you are 13 years old!

Without fail, most people will come up with a feeling and a number, eg "*I felt annoyed and it was like I was 8 and back in primary school again*", or, "*I felt embarrassed and I was back on the football pitch as a 14 year old.*"

Interestingly, our body language will reflect our emotions, so you might look like a 30 year old but be showing the temper tantrum of a 3 year old – folded arms, tapping foot and a serious pout (which may or may not be accompanied by a flounce!)

Triangle of Insight

A key part in understanding the '*cracks in the wall*' and how the past can impact on our present is a model called the 'Triangle of Insight'. This model simply describes three situations which happen simultaneously and which basically put our '*stack*' under pressure revealing the cracks.

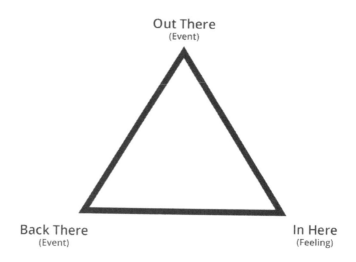

Out There
(Event)

Back There
(Event)

In Here
(Feeling)

An event in the present, eg, seeing a tiny spider, can trigger a feeling (In Here), not necessarily because of the little spider in front of us, but because our internal video camera is replaying an image of a much larger spider that was crawling across our pillow just as we woke up (Back There event). The shock of seeing the spider when we were much younger and the panic/anxiety it caused then resurfaces in the present in what may seem to others a completely irrational response. 'Out there' events can have a positive effect, eg, sitting in a restaurant. The aroma of cooking herbs can bring back pleasant memories of tavernas overlooking the sea and beautiful sunsets. You might be left feeling relaxed and calm, anticipating a tasty meal and with expectations of a lovely evening. Conversely, being ignored by the waiter when everyone else seems to be able to get his attention can trigger feelings of anger, rejection or frustration!

At work, the something happening '*out there*' might simply be that you've started to talk to your team and notice two of them whispering to each other and laughing. You begin to feel slightly insecure and the thought flashes through your mind that they might be laughing at you. At that moment '*in here*' a feeling is triggered and the feeling is accompanied by an internal voice, "*I feel stupid.*" Now, you know you are very competent and good at what you have to say but that is not what you are feeling. Why? Simply because '*back there*' your subconscious is replaying the moment when, as a 7 year old, you presented your school project on worms to the class and two kids ruined it by giggling all the way through it. Standing in front of the audience, you are really feeling like a 7 year old in a 43 year old body!   The internal terrorists are the words that come into our thoughts when the negative feelings are triggered. Let's look at dealing with them.

Nehemiah's Walls – how to deal with the Internal Terrorists

We've identified where the internal terrorists come from so now the question is how do we deal with them? One of my favourite books in the Bible is Nehemiah. It tells the story of the rebuilding of the walls of Jerusalem after it was devastated by wars. The book unfolds the story of a man, Nehemiah, who God calls to leave his high position and go back to restore the city. It recounts the challenges Nehemiah faced, how he handled them and what was going through his head at the time!

At the start of his journey of restoration Nehemiah walked around the walls of Jerusalem making a note of where the damage was, particularly of the city gates.

Jerusalem is a city with gates which, in Nehemiah's time, had names such as Mercy Gate and the Dung gate.   One of the biggest difficulties facing Nehemiah was that there were enemies of Israel who didn't want to see the city rebuilt. Some of these enemies were on the outside of the city and others were inside the city walls.

Imagine you are in the middle of Jerusalem, a city with gates that all have names. In this model, the gates are open and they have no names. The city feels vulnerable and exposed, and defenceless.

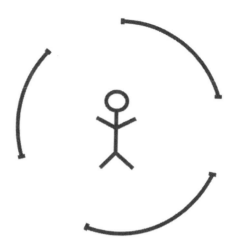

Nehemiah walked the walls of Jerusalem to see where the weaknesses were and in a similar fashion, I'd like you to 'walk your own walls' from 'gate' to 'gate'.

Think of any situation in the recent past where something hasn't quite gone to plan and you are feeling less good, less confident about yourself. Now go round the outside of the gates where there is a gap and write the word in, eg, frustrated, alone, unhappy..........., whatever you want to write – be very honest with yourself.

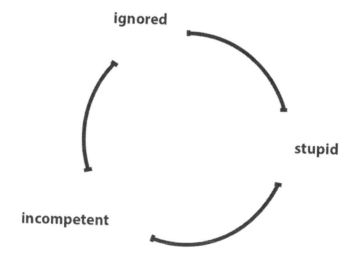

You've written down on the outside of the gate the words in your head triggered by the feelings you have when you felt less good, or less confident about yourself. Now, on the inside of the gates (inside Jerusalem:-), write down the opposite of that word.

For example, you might have written 'embarrassed' on the outside and on the inside you might want to write 'confident' or 'proud' or whatever – bearing in mind what I said earlier about communication being a meeting of meaning.

Go round all your gates, or as many as you put words on the outside, and repeat this process until all your gates have words on the inside.

Take a pen and close all the gates off so there are no gaps.

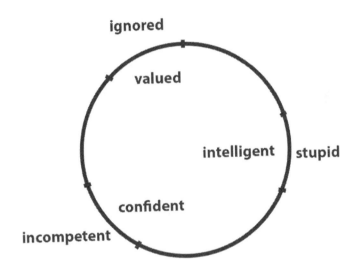

Now here is what I hope will be a fantastically freeing revelation. The truth is, the gates were never open! However, because 94-97% of us have never 'named our gates' by furnishing the inside of our gates with words of truth about who we 'be'; words about our personalities, strengths, gifts, character, - we feel vulnerable and exposed. We have nothing with which to defend ourselves against the lies of the 'enemy'! What makes it worse is that negative labelling by others can make it much more difficult for us to believe good things about ourselves.

The moment the feeling triggers the negative word and we have that in our heads, what happens is the 'internal terrorist' pops up holding a megaphone and the word rings louder in our heads. As soon as we start to pay more attention to the word that is being shouted in our heads the 'terrorist' invites the rest of his family to join in (with their various sizes of megaphone) and...the word gets louder in our heads. I can hear you saying 'This is so true'.

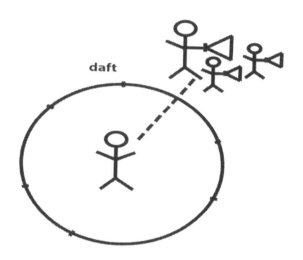

Here is the tipping point: the moment we give the terrorists our full attention, that is the point where what confidence we have goes and.....where our competencies also go (we drop our books, trip over the carpet, mumble our words – sound familiar?).

<u>Now for Victory!</u>

Look at all the words you have written inside your walls. These are words of TRUTH about you. The words on the outside are lies. Let me give you an example: you might have written 'incompetent' or 'stupid' on the outside and on the inside written 'competent' and 'capable'. You may have put 'stressed' on the outside and 'peaceful' on the inside. You need to really understand that the words on the inside are the truth about who you have been created to 'be'. The fact that that you are feeling stressed doesn't mean you are a stressful person. You might be in stressful circumstances but that doesn't make you a stressful person. You might have done something that didn't work or seemed silly BUT that doesn't make you a silly or incompetent person. I'm remembering the time when my husband poured his morning tea into the marmalade jar – he had suffered a stroke, however I'd then gone into the fridge and lo and behold there was the bag of rice I'd unpacked with the rest of the shopping!

The eyeballing technique

When the feeling triggers the word in our head and the terrorist and his family start shouting and getting our attention, the feeling gets stronger which re-reinforces our focusing on the word/s in our head. After years of practicing negative scripts in our heads 'I *feel so stupid,...but then I've always been stupid...what's the point in bothering....*' or in whatever direction our particular '*pity party*' talk takes us, we go downhill. Here is the 30 second glorious and permanent solution. The moment the feeling is triggered and the '*internal terrorist*' word pops up in your head, just eyeball the word and say 'I *refuse to receive you in my head because the truth is I am....*' and then turn your back and walk away from it.

I understand that for many people reading this, memories of abusive backgrounds, really damaging events and poor role models by those who should have nurtured and cared for you have left major cracks.

No crack is too big to be restored because no terrorist is too big to be eyeballed and dealt with - especially with Jesus holding our hand. It just takes a little courage and we're going to look at that shortly. Also, being '*cracked*' doesn't mean we haven't and won't be fabulously useful.

Waterpots and flowers

There is a story of a water bearer in India who had two large pots, each hung on the ends of a pole which he carried across his neck. One of the pots had a crack in it, while the other pot was perfect and always delivered a full portion of water. At the end of the long walk from the stream to the house, the cracked pot arrived only half full. For a full two years this went on daily, with the bearer delivering only one and a half pots full of water to his house. Of course, the perfect pot was proud of its accomplishments – perfect for which it had been made. But, the poor cracked pot was ashamed of its own imperfection, and miserable that it was able to accomplish only half of what it had been made to do.

After 2 years of what it perceived to be a bitter failure, it spoke to the water bearer one day by the stream. *"I'm ashamed of myself, and I want to apologise to you. I have been able to deliver only half my load because this crack in my side causes water to leak all the way back to your house. Because of my flaws, you have to do all of this work, and you don't get full value from your efforts,"* the pot said.

The bearer said to the pot, *"Did you notice that there were flowers only on your side of the path, but not on the other pot's side? That's because I have always known about your flaw, and planted flower seeds on your side of the path, and every day while we walk back, you've watered them. For two years I have been able to pick these beautiful flowers to decorate the table. Without you being just the way you are, there would not be this beauty to grace the house."*

Understanding the battlefield

The battle for the enemy to rob, steal and destroy who we have been made to be in Jesus Christ takes place in the mind. Thoughts impact our emotions and emotions impact our thoughts, *'Therefore, prepare your minds for action; be self-controlled; set your hope fully on the grace to be given you when Jesus Christ is revealed'* 1 Peter 1:13. However let me clarify something for those of you who struggle in standing against negative thoughts – the victory has already been won! Life on earth is not Jesus and Satan in some kind of boxing ring slogging things out until the second coming. Jesus has already won us full victory and we don't need to ever stand accused by the enemy. *'....He forgave us all our sins, having cancelled the written code, with its regulations, that was against us and that stood opposed to us; he took it away, nailing it to the cross. And having disarmed the powers and authorities, he made a public spectacle of them, triumphing over them by the cross.'* Col 2: 13-15 Hallelujah!

A little point to note

It's really good to understand and distinguish between accusations that bring us down, and God using people to bring constructive and helping change in our lives.

I've always found that when the Lord wants to highlight something in my life, eg, I'm being really impatient or not listening enough, He'll use His Word, people and circumstances to bring it to my attention. It is up to me how I respond to this. As Mark Twain said *'Denial ain't a river in Egypt!"*

<u>Sustaining the change</u>

Do you remember pictures of Singapore in June 2013 when illegal fires in Indonesia caused major smog to cover the region? Smog chokes, burns the eyes and makes it very difficult to see where you are going. When we have smog going on in our heads the effects are the same. Have you ever tried to give anything up – perhaps smoking, staying up late, chocolate, or to start something like a diet, new exercise regime or bible reading plan? How difficult was it? You probably said things like 'I *Should go to the gym'*, 'I *Must avoid chocolate'*, 'I *Ought to try to get up earlier'* or 'I've *Got to remember that reading plan'*. You're creating head SMOG.

S: I Should
M: I Must
O: I Ought to
G: I've Got to

If we use any of the above negative language then we will never do what it is we are saying we should, must, ought to or got to. The truly empowering phrase is *'I Choose To'.* Actually, this can be expanded into *'I delight in...,   I rejoice to...'* or *'What a blessing to...'* . It is incredibly freeing to say 'I *choose/rejoice to go to the gym'*, 'I *choose/am blessed not to have that slice of luscious chocolate cake'* and so on. Why? It is simply because by making a choice, we have taken control over our lives - back to 1 Peter 1:13. When we don't exercise good choices (*self-control*) our lives can feel a bit like Proverbs 25:28 *'Like a city whose walls are broke down is a man/woman without self-control'* – which brings us back to Nehemiah's walls and feeling exposed to the terrorists! SMOG is the law of works but choice is the law of grace!

'Even if you are on the right track, you will get run over if you just sit there.' Will Rogers

I'd mentioned earlier about negative labelling and how that can be embedded from an early age. From a biochemical point of view – bearing in mind the link between our minds and our bodies - did you know it takes up to 28 days to create a new neural pathway and any altered behaviour requires our 'head talk' to change as well? We need to make good choices not to reinforce negative language so we don't undermine or defeat our ability to act. For any of you who need extra encouragement to change there's a great Bob Newhart comedy sketch on Youtube called 'The Psychiatrist' – well worth watching!

'It's so important to know you can choose to feel good. Most people don't think they have that choice' Neil Simon

The Talking Triangle

This really useful tool has been put up in staffrooms, classrooms, meeting rooms – and kitchens! - as a way of reminding people that we need to respect self and others, be honest with self and others and, most importantly, make good choices in how we communicate and work with self and others.

By dealing with the *'internal terrorist'* we are able to take control of the self-talk that rattles through our heads and develop the habit of making good choices.

When we choose to use words of truth about who we *'be'*, to stand on that truth and to choose to believe it, regardless of what chaos has or is going on around us, we are able to walk in freedom and be the aroma of Christ to others. *'It is for freedom that Christ has set us free. Stand firm,*

Loving you is easy – Loving me is hard!

then, and do not let yourselves be burdened again by a yoke of slavery'
Galatians 5:1 (my emphasis again)

Reflective Exercises:

1 Draw out the city with the gates that are open and write down the words you put on the outside when you first read the chapter. Now, on the inside, write down not only the words that meant the opposite of them, but also add in the 20 (or more:-) words that described your personality, character, etc from the last chapter. Close the gates. How does seeing all those internal words make you feel?

2 Go round the 'gates' and, using two or three of the descriptive words that are most meaningful for you as your most powerful statements of truth, write those words over the gates (a bit like Jerusalem's gates all having names like 'Beautiful' etc)

3 Think of an area of your life you would like to change but it has been done with SMOG language. How would like to choose to approach this in a different way to help you actually make that change happen?

4 There is a story about how monkeys are caught: a coconut with something tasty is hung up and when the monkey comes along, it puts its hand into the coconut to get hold of the treat. As soon as the fist is clenched by holding the goodie, the monkey can't pull it's hand out of the coconut. It sees the hunters coming but won't let go and so it is caught. Is there anything that you are holding onto (it could be a bad attitude towards someone, hurt that you revisit and pick at, a judgemental mindset...- I did say we are all glorious ruins!), that grace would ask you to choose to let go of?

5 Choose two verses from the bible that really mean something to you about grace and freedom. Spend the next few days memorising and meditating on these verses. Read them at the start of the day, thank God for what they mean and that He wrote them for you to know how to live. Think about ways in which you can practise the truth of these verses moment by moment.

6 Think of times that someone has shared something with you that has maybe been hard to hear but has been a blessing. Did you know God was using this situation? What did you learn from it? Think about your relationship with God – did this situation draw you closer to God? Why?

7 You might want to include these thoughts in your journal so that you can see how the Lord is intensely interested in the fine details of your life:-)

Bible verses worth exploring:

1 In John 8, Jesus is having a conversation with some very hard-hearted people who have trouble listening or understanding what He is saying. Jesus then makes a comment about the devil in verse 44 '...*He was a murderer from the beginning, not holding to the truth, for there is no truth in him. When he lies, he speaks his native language, for he is a liar and the father of lies*'. If you had the choice between truth and lies – what would you choose to believe? Why? For some people, it is easier to believe lies as that would mean they didn't have to make uncomfortable choices and get their lives in order. If that is you, you might want to choose to get your hand out of that coconut you've been holding onto so dearly!

2 Matthew 7: 24-25 What are the short-term and long-term effects of making wise choices?

3 Jeremiah 15:16 and Jeremiah 17:7-9 What image do these verses conjure up in your mind? Think about the individual phrases in the verses – write down any thoughts. It can be quite interesting to see how what is written down can be quite powerful and this is one way that God speaks to us – through words and thoughts in our head that seem to be very encouraging and uplifting\o/

4 2 Corinthians 1:21-22 Can you read this verse and find any loopholes about how confident we can be in God's hold on our lives? For those who aren't sure if they have given God 'ownership' of their lives here's a helpful little prayer.

Dear Lord, I know I've done many things that don't please you. I've lived my life without you and for myself and I want to say I'm sorry. I want to start a new life and I believe Jesus died on the cross and rose from the dead for me, to save me. He did what I couldn't do for myself. I ask you Lord to forgive me and come into my heart by your Holy Spirit, take control of my life and help me to grow in my love, friendship and relationship with you. Help me to live every day for you. Thank you, Amen.

You may find it helpful to look at 1 John 5:11-12 and also Ephesians 1:13-14. You might like to memorise them as well:-)

For reflection:

I AM

I was regretting the past and fearing
the future
Suddenly my Lord was speaking
My Name is I AM

He paused: I waited: He continued

When you live in the past, with its mistakes and regrets,
It is hard; I am not there
My Name is not I WAS

When you live in the future, with its
problems and fears,
It is hard: I am not there:
My Name is not I WILL BE

When you live in this moment it
is not hard

I am here
My Name is
I AM

Helen Mallicoat

CHAPTER 3   Becoming an Influencer

So here we are. We've eyeballed the terrorists and have stacked our gates with lots of truthful words about who God has made us to be. We've chosen to believe these words even if we don't always feel they are true – remembering that faith isn't a hormonal condition! We look around us and want to make a positive impact on the world. There's a wonderful quote from the film Jurassic Park where a scientist (Dr Ian Malcom) describes Chaos Theory.....'*A butterfly can flap its wings in Peking and in Central Park you get rain instead of sunshine.*' Basically, whatever we do or say will have an impact on the lives of those around us.

One model of understanding how we interact with other people is Transactional Analysis (TA). I've included this section on Transactional Analysis because it is really useful in helping us grow into being who God has made us to be. The more we understand what makes us '*tick*', the easier it is to let go of unhealthy patterns of behaviour. This in turn helps reinforce our ability to make healthy choices which will keep us moving forward.

Eric Berne explained that the human personality is made up of three 'ego' states which he called the Parent, Adult and Child. The ego being our sense of self-esteem or self-importance.

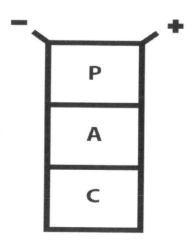

Remember how earlier I said that from the moment we are born we video everything? We may be standing in a room with some friends, however, each person carries the 'Child' inside (with that large volume of film footage with associated feelings). Each person will also carry a 'Parental' voice (this is the voice from a strong older figure – it could be a carer, teacher, parent, older sibling etc) which can be positive or negative.

Put simply, each of the Ego states tends to have it's own kind of statement of intent:

Parent Ego State – Do what I say
Adult Ego State – Lets agree what to do
Child Ego State - I need help or I want my way

The Parent Ego State is our ingrained voice of authority through which we have absorbed patterns of behaviour, learning and attitudes from when we were young. Some of these older 'parental' figures can be real people but also fictional as well ranging from the benevolent Father Christmas (who will reward 'good' children) to the scary Bogey Man lurking under the bed! The 'parental' influence can be:

Nurturing - Nurturing (positive) and Spoiling (negative).
Controlling - Structuring (positive) and Critical (negative).

The Child Ego State tends to be expressed physically, (emotionally sad expressions, despair, temper tantrums, whining voice, rolling eyes, shrugging shoulders, teasing, delight, laughter, speaking behind hand, raising hand to speak, squirming and giggling), and verbally (baby talk, I wish, I dunno, I want, I'm gonna, I don't care, oh no, not again, things never go right for me, worst day of my life, bigger, biggest, best, many superlatives, words to impress). The Child influence can be:

Adapted - Co-operative (positive) and Compliant/Resistant (negative).
Free - Spontaneous (positive) and Immature (negative)

The Adult Ego State expresses itself physically by being attentive, interested, straight-forward, tilted head, non-threatening and non-threatened. It's verbal expression is through - why, what, how, who, where and when, how much, in what way, comparative expressions, reasoned statements, true, false, probably, possibly, I think, I realise, I see,

I believe, in my opinion. The Adult remains as a single entity, representing an 'accounting' function or mode, which can draw on the resources of both Parent and Child.

"This is all very interesting." I hear you say, *"but where are you going with this Libby?"* Imagine the scenario; you have gone to meet with some friends and everyone has arrived before you and started to order their meal. You are left to sit down in the chair at the end of the table next to two people very engrossed in a very funny conversation.

As you sit down, one of the people (let's call her Meg) turns to you and smiles then says to the person opposite her, in what you think is a sarcastic tone of voice, *'Well here's Susan.'*

At this point (and this all happens in a flash!), the perceived negative parental tone of that voice triggers the child's video camera and you feel so inept and as though you are 6 years old arriving late, with your always tardy family, for Auntie Annie's birthday party – and she was not amused. What happens next is you feel yourself slipping out of being an adult into – at an emotional level - being a child with all the accompanying body language and verbal script. *'Well it wasn't my fault the taxi was late ...whine whine'.* The problem is, if someone slips into child mode, what does it force the other person to become – you've got it - the Parent! So now at this lovely dinner out, we have one woman who now feels like a 6 year old because of her own assumption about what someone meant with that perceived negative tone of voice, and, to make matters worse, the other woman is now moving into being the corrective or nurturing *'parent'*, and as at this stage we're not quite sure which way she will go – a drama unfolds.

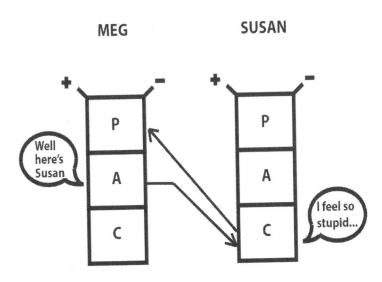

I am sure you can think of instances at work, socially or in family situations which demonstrate these dynamics.

There might be someone at work or in your family who always takes control of any situation even though you are more than capable of sorting it out yourself and leaves you feeling somewhat inept. Or, you know someone who is quite aloof and needing attention for no apparent reason. To be honest, all of these little 'control dramas' tend to sap everyone's energy except for the person driving the drama. They are having all the benefits of caffeine without having to drink it!

Control Dramas

Along with finding ourselves shifting to feeling like a 'child' or conversely being pushed into 'Parent', we also get involved in various little 'control dramas' – patterns of behaviour learned as we grow through childhood from those older than us (parents, carers, older siblings etc). Control dramas tend to range between Aggressive and Passive through the spectrum of Intimidator, Interrogator, Aloof and Poor me. Have a look at the control dramas listed below.

- Intimidator - On the verge of exploding, threatening, strict, gave orders, inflexible, angry, self-centered, made you feel afraid.
- Interrogator - Probes to see what you are/were doing; critical,

undermining, needling, infallible logic, sarcasm, monitored you. Can be skeptical, sarcastic, self-righteous, perfectionist.

- Aloof - tends to be distant, busy, away from home, not too interested in your life, unresponsive, secretive, and preoccupied.
- Poor me - Always sees the negative, looks for problems, always talking about being busy or tired, makes you feel guilty for not solving their problems. Draws attention to themselves by sighing, trembling, crying, and adopting a 'victim' stance

Here are a couple of questions you might like to think about:

a) Which of these control dramas did your dominant 'parent' best fit?
b) Which one do you best fit?

The healthiest ego state is Adult – Adult Ego because it helps facilitate agreement and understanding.

So the person who knows and understands themselves, has dealt with their internal terrorists and loves who they 'be', is free from having their 'buttons' pressed by others and can stay as the Adult. A good example of this would be to go back to the ladies meeting up for the meal and rerun this in another way. Let's imagine Susan has arrived late and Meg has come out with her comment. However this time, as Meg says ' Well here's Susan', she notices Susan's face and body language. Susan has her eyes down (means I feel defeated or intimidated), crosses her arms (means self comforting) and then reaches for the menu and begins stroking her hair (means fantasy – I wish I was anywhere but here!). This is where Meg, holding on to the Adult and resisting the urge to be the Parent (poor you or pull yourself together), and knowing that two of her own qualities are kindness and hospitality can save the situation from being a disaster. Meg turns to Susan and giving her full attention, smiles and says something along the lines of 'Susan, it's great to see you – it must have been tricky getting the kids sorted before heading out. We've all just started so that is perfect timing. Now tell us about what you've been up to this past week...'

'No-one can make you feel bad about yourself unless you give them permission to do so' Eleanor Roosevelt

Loving you is easy – Loving me is hard!

Some interesting info

When we are interacting with others, we see and feel what is going on as well as hear what is said. About 7% of meaning is in the words spoken. 38% of meaning is paralinguistic (the way that the words are said), and, 55% is in facial expression. We read body language incredibly quickly and that is what informs our reactions.

Each ego state has an entire system of thought, feeling and behaviour from which we interact with other people. When we communicate with each other 'transactions' take place between the different ego states. TA practitioners identify which ego states people are transacting from and by observing the process, can stop unhelpful patterns of response and build in healthy ones. This obviously facilitates very effective communication skills because not only are negative reactions being replaced with positive ones but the 'games' played out through dysfunctional behavioural patterns are also stopped. Berne labeled some of the games people with names like "I'm only trying to help you", "Why don't you, yes but," amongst others – do these ring a bell? By recognizing that in childhood, and as we grow up, we can subconsciously make self-limiting decisions about ourselves as a survival mechanism, we can free ourselves up to make healthy changes.

Some more about onions

Remember back in Chapter 1 I talked about the Onion or Shrek model which looked at our core passion – our influence. Knowing my core passion means I can consciously take that positive influence with me into any situation. If Meg's core passion was to make people feel happy or loved, then that would motivate her to speak thoughtfully and kindly to Susan. Someone else whose core passion was determination might get the same outcomes in the conversation but use different words to achieve that. For example, they might say 'Susan, it's great to see you – you are really organized in getting the kids sorted before heading out, and, your timing is perfect.'

When someone prays the 'prayer of faith' and enters into a relationship with God as their Heavenly Father, if they have had a bad or poor relationship with their own father, it is very hard to try to visualise how God can be any different. Not only that, but how we act around people in everyday life is carried over into how we tend to relate to Father, Son and Holy Spirit. Just as we have learned to deal with our *'internal terrorists'* and trust in truth, so we also need to get to know the truth about who our Heavenly Father is. It is so important to get to know God. This comes from getting to know what He says about Himself in the Bible, spending time with Him (we'll look at that in the Chapter about the gardens of God), and experiencing His presence every day. Take truths from the Bible, see them prove true in experience and discover the Holy Spirit teaching you new things.

The Bride

It's probably a good idea to mention that the unhealthy dynamics that can come about through someone being the *'aggressive child'* or *'controlling parent'* can be just as evident in churches. For most people churches are where we expect to grow in our faith and are seen as 'safe' places. Abuse, when it happens, can be devastating. Often it is just a very small minority, just one or two people who cause the damage. Sadly the ripples of the emotional and spiritual damage just spread and spread. I remember the comment from a pastor's wife who was talking about some of the difficult people in their church. When someone commented that sheep can bite, her reply was *'Some of ours have got rabies!'* There are churches where the leadership have controlled and abused the sheep, or 'sheep' have made life very difficult for their leaders. *'The Subtle Power of Spiritual Abuse'* by David Johnson and Jeff Vanvonderen and *'People of the Lie'* by M Scott Peck are excellent reference books.

On the whole, the church is made up of wonderfully ordinary communities of forgiving and forbearing people. God sees all those who love Him, coming together to form His Bride. May I encourage you to remember that in any church, the majority desire to see the church grow in maturity, joy, and grace. When problems arise the Lord is not taken by surprise. He sees everything. He just asks us to draw near to Him, use discernment and wisdom, stand firm in who He has made us to be, and He will deal with everything, in His way and His timings.

Parrots and Turkeys

A young man named Jim received a parrot as gift. The parrot had a bad attitude and an even worse vocabulary. The bird did nothing but badmouth or swear, despite every effort by Jim to change the bird's attitude by speaking kindly, or giving it particularly tasty food. Finally, totally fed up, Jim shouted at the parrot which not only yelled back, but did so with very choice language. Jim shook the parrot and it then got madder and even worse language came out. In desperation, Jim grabbed the parrot and put it in the freezer. For a few minutes the parrot squawked and kicked and screamed, and then suddenly, there was silence. After a minute or so of this unearthly stillness, Jim opened the freezer door. The parrot quietly stepped onto Jim's outstretched arm and said *'I'd like to apologise for my rudeness and bad language. I am very sorry for my bad attitude and how I've behaved and I will never again repeat this behaviour'*. Jim was totally taken aback and just as he was about to ask the parrot what had caused this remarkable turnaround, the parrot asked *'May I ask what the turkey did?'*

Changing from the inside

I love this particular verse: 2 Corinthians 3:18 *'And we all, with unveiled face, beholding the beauty of the Lord, are being changed into His likeness. This comes from the Lord who is the Spirit'*. Why do I love it? Because it shows we are being changed from the inside out, not by working at it like a peak performance athlete trying to stay on top by sheer effort, but by the indwelling Holy Spirit. What a relief! No matter what your background or experience of life, the best is yet to come.

Talking about being changed, we've all been in a situation where someone has been really impatient/tetchy/critical/(substitute any negative word you like) and when they see the look on your face say *'well that's just the way I am'*, or, *'I'm expressing my inner self'*. I remember a good friend who had a fiery temper saying one day that she'd realised she was *'indulging in the luxury'* of letting go of emotional control – at which point she stopped losing her temper! We're told that the Holy Spirit produces this kind of fruit in our lives; love, joy, peace, patience, kindness, goodness and faithfulness, so when someone says they are getting, for example, more impatient, the question is why are they choosing impatience rather than patience?

"If we claim to be without sin, we deceive ourselves and the truth is not in us. If we confess our sins, he is faithful and just and will forgive us our sins and purity us from all unrighteousness." I John 1:8-10

45

What are we aiming for?

Have you ever bought something to wear and tried it on in the shop, brought it home, put it on again and when you looked in the mirror, realised that something wasn't quite as you'd thought it was; a bit too big, not quite the right colour or it had a flaw you hadn't noticed in the shop. The advantage of seeing where something isn't quite right is that we can rectify it – in the case of clothes we can take them back.

This is a bit like how we can see ourselves against the mirror of God's character. The beauty of getting to know the truth about what God is like acts like a mirror for us in seeing what we are like, eg, impatient against God's characteristic of being amazingly patient. Now please note, this is not a comparison competition where we feel a failure or diminished because we lack something or see imperfection in ourselves. Rather, it is more what I call the Jack and the Beanstalk perspective.

Jack and the Beanstalk

Do you remember the story of Jack and the Beanstalk where the bean was planted and Jack then started climbing up the beanstalk to get to the top. This is a bit, for me anyway, like living the Christian life. I start struggling to climb up the first step to the castle, I pull and stretch and get up the first step and go up the next one, then the next one – getting more and more tired as I expend more energy – and then finally stop part way up to draw breath. I turn round and look down at where I've climbed up from and am amazed at how I've come. Everything looks different from this place and I feel quite chuffed (pleased) with myself. Then, I feel this tapping on my shoulder and I turn round and look up, only to realise that there is still quite a way to go.

Isn't that so like growing as a person – we come so far and have learned so much, and yet there will always be room to grow even more.

'I'm such an optimist I'd go after Moby Dick in a rowing boat and take the tartar sauce with me' Zig Ziglar

When we are out of breath and realizing there are more steps ahead of us isn't it great either to be an optimist or to have friends who are!

Loving you is easy – Loving me is hard!

Whether it is family, friends or colleagues, we can look at the healthy and positive attributes in the people we most admire and learn from them as well. If you've just had your first child it's great when you know people with older children who you see as great role models. I don't know about you but I learn best from seeing something being practised rather than reading the theory from a detached distance.

Reflective Exercises

1 Think about some situations that caused you to react in a particular way – could be happy, irritated.... Now thinking of each situation ask yourself the question: 'Why did I react like that?' The answers to this will help you understand what presses your buttons. How would you have preferred to react (am thinking of something that is positive rather than 'I'd like to have thrown a custard pie in their face!)?

2 Ask someone to be your partner and stand facing one another. Decide who is going to talk first. The person who is to talk first has to talk for one minute on why they are amazing. The person who is listening...and this is important...has to give no facial or verbal response at all (if you find you want to laugh or say something, just look away or fold your arms and ignore the 'speaker'). Time this for one minute then swop over and repeat this in reverse. As the speaker, how did you feel when you were getting no response? Why? For the listener, how did it feel when you had to give no response? Why?

3 Think of the exercise you've just done – is there anything you've learned about your communication style and the possible impact it might have on other types of people? What about the reverse ie how other people's communication style makes you feel? Write down some words that describe your way of talking with other people eg humorous, empathetic, impassive...Write down one thing you might like to work on when talking/listening?

4 Think of people who have been great role models for you in different areas of your life and at different times. How have they influence you and how has that benefitted you?

5 If you could leave a legacy for the next generation that would equip them for life, what would you want that to be and why?

Loving you is easy – Loving me is hard!

Bible verses worth exploring:

1 Romans 8:1 and John 13:34   Do you ever listen to the radio, read the papers and watch TV only to realise we are listening to one set of opinions after another. Commentators pass opinions on everything and in their own eyes, theirs is the right opinion. I listened to two Professors of Economics, one saying why Scotland couldn't possibly go independent and the other saying why Scotland could. Both were speaking the truth – from their point of view. Isn't it a wonderful thing just to get on with being kind to others!

2 Titus 2:11 and Titus 3:4   Have some time just thinking about these verses and what Jesus brought with Him when He came to live among us. Reflect on how Jesus has ministered these truths to you. You may want to take just one aspect of a verse and ask the Lord to help this become part of your ministry to others.

3 Galatians 5:13-15 Remember the coconut and the monkey? If there are people who have hurt or irritated you or you have challenges with different personality types you might like to think of talking with the Lord about it, asking forgiveness for holding onto any attitudes (even if you were in the right!). Bless the people from your heart and pray for the Lord to watch over them. Pray intelligently about any needs they might have, ask for the windows of Heaven to open up and for the Lord to provide all they might need. You will be amazed at how generous your heart will become and you will get to the point where you will really mean everything you are praying...and you will be amazed at how free and blessed you will be in return.

For Reflection:

'ANYWAY'

People are often unreasonable, illogical, and self-centred
Forgive them anyway.
If you are kind, people may accuse you of selfish, ulterior motives,
Be kind anyway.

If you are successful, you will win some false friends and some true enemies;
Succeed anyway.
If you are honest and frank, people may cheat you;
Be honest and frank anyway.

What you spend years building, someone could destroy overnight;
Build anyway.
If you find serenity and happiness, they may be jealous;
Be happy anyway.

The good you do today, people will often forget tomorrow;
Do good anyway.
Give the world the best you have, and it may never be enough;
Give the world the best you have anyway.

You see, in the final analysis, it is between you and God;
It was never between you and them anyway.

Words of Mother Theresa of Calcutta

Chapter 4 – Dealing with anxiety and fear

'Some day my boat will come in and with my luck I'll be at the airport'
Graffiti

Do you every worry about anything? It might be that you are on the wrong path in life or that you will miss the bus, your hair will fall out or the dental checkup will reveal the need for several fillings!

Whatever it is, big or small, it is those 'terrorists' creating anxiety and fear that can hold us back from taking decisions, making healthy choices and loving who the Lord has made us to be – with all the blessings that go with that. We can have dealt with our internal terrorists but still be assailed by worries and anxieties on a daily basis because there seems to be so much in life to worry about. We grow up embedding patterns of responding to situations (internal terrorists, Parent/Adult/Child), which also includes developing patterns in handling anxiety and fear. We might have grown up with parental/adult role models who reinforced negative messages eg *'Now if you are on your own at the bus stop at night you need to be careful in case someone tries to abduct you (you could also substitute murder, attack, beat you up!),'*

When our son was about 6, there was a school programme designed to warn children of the danger of strangers. If they didn't know someone, they weren't to linger or talk with them but to run off. One day, Peter came rushing through the front door with a look of pride on his face. He'd been walking home when two people started to walk beside him and he'd turned and cried *'Strangers, strangers!'* and hot-footed it up the road – leaving two very bemused pensioners behind! There is a difference between good advice and creating angst.

'Never take anxiety or worry to bed with you. They will snore all night'.
- Jennifer Mark, health writer.

Tsunamis and sharks

The availability of information via the internet, television, phones etc gives us access to information that can be helpful but also create anxiety. What adds into the melting pot is our imagination. Imagination is a wonderful thing – you just have to watch children playing to see imagination in action. Children can spend hours on a rainy day sailing the seas as pirates battling with dinosaurs, just using a cardboard box, some homemade pirate hats, various stuffed toys and anything else that comes to hand. Everything can become anything. As we grow up our imagination continues to feed our thinking. For example, if you live by the sea and then saw the terrible film footage of the Japanese tsunami, you might imagine what it might be like if a tsunami happened where you live. Now you might live thousands of miles from an earthquake zone, or high up above any wave damage level, but, it doesn't stop your imagination playing out the scene. Then, having imagined the wave, your mind then moves onto the loss of life, damage to your house, how you would react to family dying and so on. Our emotional energy is consumed in responding to an imaginary situation and it is exhausting.

When we were on honeymoon in Oban, we went to the local cinema and watched 'Jaws' – it made me very nervous about going in the sea for a swim even though there are no white sharks in Scotland. Actually, the sea is pretty chilly so the shark was only partly the reason!

God can only give us grace for the reality of a situation we are actually in at a particular moment. He can't give us grace for something we are imagining might happen. Let me show you a little model which I find really useful.

**FUTURE
PAST
-ve**

**FUTURE
PAST
+ve**

TRUST | HOPE
PEACE | JOY

Journey of Life

In the picture, let's say the person sitting in the middle of the 'vehicle' is you. We journey along the road of life and with us we carry our past and our thoughts for the future, both of which can have positive and negative connotations. We may have very fond memories of our past which make us look forward to more good things in the future. Conversely, we might have had negative experiences in our past that make us anxious about our future. For example, if we remember really struggling at swimming lessons and not being able to swim without armbands, we might get anxious if friends suggest a day's whitewater rafting! Negative experiences inform our list of 'pain' values while positive experiences inform our list of 'joy' values. Whatever value is strongest will determine how we respond to a situation.

Imagine being asked to go for a ride in a hot air balloon. Because your top joy value is 'adventure', you think fantastic that will be great fun. However, as you tell friends what you are going to be doing, a couple of comments come your way along the lines of 'I heard about about someone who fell out the balloon just as it was going up – how embarrassing', or 'It would be so embarrassing if you suddenly changed your mind and wanted to jump out ha ha'. It so happens that your top pain value is 'embarrassment', so while you really would like to go on the hot air balloon trip, your pain value (being stronger than your joy value in this case) will influence you to back out and say 'No' to the trip. Someone else whose joy value is stronger than their pain value will go in the hot air trip regardless.

Sliding into anxiety and fear

What most commonly happens – and this refers back to the 'terrorists' – is that when we think of something we might be looking forward to, such as a holiday, or a meal with friends or a days fishing, if we've had a negative experience in the past, that can completely change the direction our wheel goes in. We might think about planning a holiday but then the thought enters our head 'That last flight was really bumpy and it made me scared' or 'The food in the last resort was awful and it was too noisy'. This little thought triggers a feeling of distrust 'I'm not sure if I can trust the tour operators brochure'. This sense of distrust starts to unsettle us and we begin to think of other things that might also go wrong and we feel a distinct lack of peace about the holiday! The moment our peace starts to go, so does our joy. It's not possible to be joyful when we are worried as anxiety becomes an overriding driver. The loss of joy immediately impacts on our hopes for a great holiday, after all, how can we hope to have a great holiday when we don't trust the operator, we've had bad experiences and we fear that what happened in the past will simply repeat itself.

By this point, this little terrorist thought has grabbed hold of you and you're sliding into the cycle of anxiety and fear which will take you nowhere except backwards.

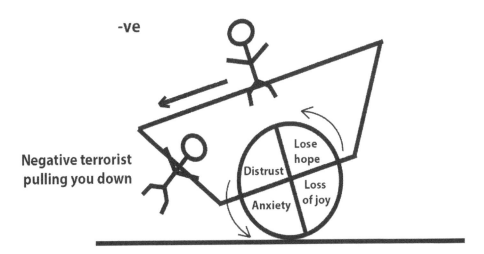

Sliding into Hope

Picture something you are hoping to do. It might be to go on holiday, meet a friend for a meal, spend a day fishing or whatever. As you think about what you are 'HOPE'ing to do, your mind begins visualising what that would be like - chilling out on the beach with that soporific warmth and sunshine, a fabulously tasty meal with room for a special dessert afterwards, the sun playing on the river and large salmon leaping onto your hook. The effects of thinking about what you are hoping for trigger feelings of contentment and JOY. A sense of certainty settles inside you and you feel a sense of PEACE that what you are hoping for will actually come to pass. The peace you feel reinforces a sense of TRUST that everything will all work out – even if you are not quite sure exactly how or when.

Trust then reinforces the sense of Hope and the Cycle of Hope runs forward, enabling you to weather circumstances and the ups and downs of the road you are running along. You expect good to win through in the end.

The positive embracement of expecting good to work out in the end helps make your cup always half full. For a Christian, the hub of the wheel is Christ as the centre. When we stay centred on Christ, our hope based on who He is (our Saviour, refuge, provider, Rock, kindness, mercy.) and the truths and promises in the Bible eg 'Surely God is my salvaton; I will trust and not be afraid. The Lord, the Lord himself, is my strength and my defense, he has become my salvation' Isaiah 12:2, we can only go one way....forward.

Staying centred on truth

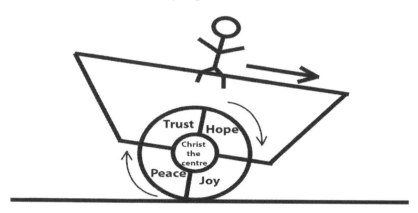

I should tell you that it was reading Romans 15:13 when this Cycle of Hope vs Anxiety and Fear leapt off the page, so whilst I've applied my creative thinking to this, the originator of the truth behind this model is... God!

Reflective Exercises

1 Write down a list of your top five 'pain' values. Now write down a list of your top five 'joyful' values.

2 Look at your pain values and decide how you would like to change how you respond to them – it might be writing a simple sentence like *'I choose to ignore that...'*

3 Think about what is at the centre of your life. Does that give you stability or not? Why?

4 Look at everything around you. Write down or share with someone one good thing that is in your life today. It might be the way the sun shone on a raindrop, your teeth felt squeaky clean after brushing them, you didn't have to wait for the bus or someone said something nice to you. Think of how *'good'* feels.

5 For one hour focus on the good things in your life (once you have thought of something just file it away but be aware of what you had thought about). See if you can keep coming back to that good thought from time to time as a reminder that there are good things in your life.

6 See if you can find an opportunity to say something kind and positive to someone else. It might be thanking the girl at the checkout for her help, or commenting on a colleague's colour of clothes – it doesn't matter how small or mundane, it just needs to be something that shows a genuine interest in the other person. How did it make you feel? How did the other person respond?

Bible verses worth exploring:

1 2 Corinthians 5:17 – 21   Look at some of the phrases in these verses that are particularly meaningful for you. Take one phrase or word at a time and see where your thoughts take you. You might like to add these thoughts to your journal.

2 1 Thessalonians 5:16   It's not easy to be joyful in 'all' circumstances. How can keeping your heart and mind centred on Christ help. You might like to think of circumstances where the Lord has really helped and journal these as reminders of His walking with you all the days of your life.

3 Romans 15:13 It might be worth exploring other verses or passages in the bible that talk about 'overflow' – it conjures up images of water flowing, rivers, waterfalls, springs. See where your exploration takes you. Is there anything that the Lord might speak to you about in your journey of exploration.

4 Jeremiah 15:16 Is there a relationship between knowing the truths in God's word and hope? Reflect on what it might mean to 'bear your name'.

5 Philippians 4:6,7 What does this promise ask us to do and what is the guaranteed answer (remember the monkey and the coconut!).

6 Deuteronomy 33:12   How wonderful!

For Reflection:

Good Morning from God:

Good morning, I'm God. I will be handling all your problems today. Please remember I DO NOT need your help.

If the devil happens to deliver a situation to you that you cannot handle, DO NOT attempt to resolve it. Kindly put it in the SFJTD (something for Jesus to do) box. It will be addressed in MY time, not yours.

Once the matter is placed in the box, DO NOT hold on to it or attempt to remove it. Holding on or removal will delay the resolution of your problem. If it is a situation that you think you are capable of handling, please consult me in prayer to be sure it is the proper resolution.

Because I do not sleep nor slumber, there is no need for you to lose any sleep. Rest my child.

If you need to contact me, I am only a prayer away.

Chapter 5 – Spending time in the garden

The Genesis of the Gardens

In the previous chapters we've looked at how to become authentically confident through learning to enjoy who we are made to *'be'*. We've explored understanding ourselves and other people, along with focussing mindfully on good things. The question is why is this so important not just for ourselves but for God?

The Lord has gone to great lengths to restore our relationship with Him and His desire is that this is known, understood and experienced by all peoples in all generations. It all started in the garden of Eden in Genesis. The very first thing that God did with Adam (after naming animals, creating seas and all the other bits and pieces!) was to spend time with him in that garden.

Ever since everything went pear-shaped, and we were driven out of the garden because of Adam and Eve sinning, God has done everything He can to enable us to get back into having "garden time" with Him. Sin is part of our fallen nature so God sent His Son Jesus to take the penalty for our sins and bring us back into relationship with Him. He's given us the Holy Spirit, angels to watch over us, His Word to give us a clear route map and a beautiful world to live in. He listens to our every thought and prayer and takes delight in answering them (though not always quite how or when we expect!). He is always present even if He sometimes feels very close and other times far away.

You and I, along with countless others, have survived experiences which have ranged from the joyous to those which have riven our hearts with grief and sorrow. As Rudyard Kipling once said *"Gardens are not made by singing 'O how beautiful,' and sitting in the shade"*.

One day this scripture really caught my attention: *"At the place where Jesus was crucified there was a garden , and in the garden a new tomb, in which no-one had ever been laid"* John 19:41

The mention of *'a garden'* in this verse is accompanied with a tomb. As I reflected on this verse, I realised for Jesus, the tomb was a place of rest but also the place of resurrection power. The only way He could enter that garden was by totally yielding everything. He had to let go of His life, His spirit, His reputation, other people's expectations and much more. He chose to let go and in so doing, He entered that garden which His Heavenly Father had prepared for Him and in which His Father was present. Jesus went in dead, spent time with His Heavenly Father and came out alive! Now we can have that same experience because Jesus is *"....the pioneer and perfector of faith. For the joy set before Him, He endured the cross, scorning its shame, and sat down at the right hand of the throne of God."* Hebrews 12:2

This wonderful theme of the gardens of God comes through the Bible time and time again. We see how, regardless of whatever circumstance people found themselves in, God made an inner garden available to them and where He was waiting to spend time with them. Those who took time to enter came out refreshed, supported, encouraged and strong enough to face whatever was going on externally. The garden is the place of resurrection and transformation.

"One can never consent to creep when one feels an impulse to soar." - Helen Keller

The Garden of Trust

"The gem cannot be polished without friction, nor man perfected without trials." Chinese proverb

When I was a very young Christian, I was inspired by the apostle Paul's imagery of the Christian life being like an athlete running the race to receive the prize. This imagery was reinforced by that wonderful film 'Chariots of Fire'. In the film there is a scene where Eric Liddell trips and falls over in a race. The other athletes press on and it seems as though for Eric the race is over. Nonetheless, he picks himself up and starts to run after the others. Incredibly he not only catches up but overtakes them to win the race. As he passed the finishing line ahead of the others, I felt my spirit rise up with pride! God had done something marvellous. I always imagined that the *"cloud of witnesses"* (Hebrews 12:1) would include people like Eric Liddell, full of power, commitment and endurance, or George Mueller of Bristol - what faith! Theresa of Avila - what a prayer life! Corrie ten Boom - what grace! and countless others known and unknown, who faced trials and tribulations yet pressed forward with God until they died.

It seemed to me that such people had done something with their lives to demonstrate their appreciation of what God had done for them. When I first asked Christ into my life, I was spiritually guided by a wonderful couple, Charles and Anne Clayton. They patiently listened to my numerous questions - I would have A4 sheets of questions arising from things I read in the bible! They taught me how to get into the Word, have times with God every day, do bible study, memorise scripture and pray. I was consumed with zeal for the Lord. I set myself to give back to the Lord everything I could in order to please Him.

By the end of my first year (somewhat pooped from trying to convert the world!), I realised with a jolt that, whilst my knowledge of and activities to do with spiritual things had increased dramatically, I didn't actually know the Lord any better at the end of the year than I had at the beginning. It gradually dawned on me that my relationship with God ran along the lines of - *"Yes Lord, I know I live by grace but don't You need some help organising Your church? You've got it all planned out? Are You sure? It doesn't seem too healthy to me! Well I'm managing to fit in extra times of meditation on top of bible study, prayer and reading all that good literature. Oh! You'd really rather we spent some time sitting in the garden - have I missed something here Lord!"* I hadn't really grasped how strongly God wanted me to make space in my life so that He and I could be intimate friends.

Whenever we find some space in our lives there can be a tendency to fill it up with activities. Phrases echoing around our minds like *'...a man reaps what he sows"* (Gal 6:7) or *"Go to the ant you sluggard."* (Prov 6:6) often tip the balance between taking time to be with God and guiltily feeling we are not doing enough to please Him. It is as if we feel that being close to God won't be enough for Him. And I also suspect that deep down we fear that God Himself won't be enough for us.

Now Genesis gives us a marvellous picture of God creating but also having time to sit and rest in the garden. It is fascinating to observe that from that time of being banished from the garden re-entering garden space with God has been mankind's greatest struggle. In Isaiah we read *"This is what the Sovereign Lord, ... says: In repentance and rest is your salvation, in quietness and trust is your strength, but you would have none of it.*

Loving you is easy – Loving me is hard!

...Yet the Lord longs to be gracious to you..." (Is 30:15,18).

Why is it we find it easier, despite all the stress, to try and develop strategies and lifestyles that we think will please God and satisfy other people's expectations? Why can't we simply let go of those things that keep us at the garden gate, peering into a sacred and wonderful space where God Himself is sitting and waiting for our company? We know it to be true and yet even that isn't enough to get us to open the gate and go in!

It brings to mind Revelation 2:3-4 *"You have persevered and have endured hardships for my name.....Yet I hold this against you; you have forsaken your first love."*

The answer seems to lie in the doubts that assail our minds about the trustworthiness of God - the same doubt sown by Satan in that first garden *"Did God really say..."* (Gen 3:1). However, the doubt sown in Eden about the results of eating of the fruit of a particular tree has spread to sow seeds of doubt in every aspect of the relationship between the Creator and His creation.

I am sure many of you can identify with some of the following doubts: *"I know God thinks I'm beautiful but I have real doubts about my nose/baldness/_____"* Please fit in whatever you know you'd like to add! Or, *"I know I'll reap what I sow but God can't mean that in this frustrating job, I must have misread His will to be here in the first place."* It is almost as if for every promise of blessing that the Lord has given us, we readily slip into the *"Did God really say...?"* way of thinking, especially if things don't seem to be going smoothly. At the same time we are not too unhappy about this as we think we are saving ourselves from spiritual pride! In our endeavours to be thinking people, wise and knowledgeable, we seem to have lost the ability to reason with our hearts.

As Albert Einstein said, *"We should take care not to make the intellect our god; it has, of course, powerful muscles, but no personality."*

We can get so bogged down in how we perform for God that we lose sight of the pain that God feels for us in our struggles. Longing for us to come into the inner garden and share ourselves with Him, He sees us stuck at the gate and He is saying, *"Come through! You are breaking my heart."*

It's time to go through the gate and into the garden – every day. He wants us to trust Him and enter the rest of faith so that we can be intimate with Him, and Jesus, who lived in our humanity, shows us how to do just that.

It is ironic that we find it difficult to put our trust in God for all sorts of things - a new job, a marriage partner, financial needs etc, but I wonder if you have ever considered how much more difficult it must have been for God to put His plans for Jesus into human hands?

Jesus would be born in a stable, but would the donkey get there in time? Murderers were after the baby but what if Joseph thought the dream about going to Egypt was that extra falafel he'd had for supper? Old Simeon might have dropped the baby in the temple, and Mary, knowing the prophecies about the coming Messiah, might either try and push Jesus ahead of God's plan or, even more naturally as a mother, overprotect Him from what she suspected might lie ahead? When Jesus spoke in the temple as a young boy what was to prevent some impressed talent-spotters clubbing together to give the boy a scholarship to Pharisee Theological College?

You can see the possible pitfalls all the way through until Jesus is faced with the last place of trust - the cross, and, as with all issues of trust, it cost a great deal. People had heard and seen evidence of Jesus' trust in His Father. There were people standing at the cross who had had some of those loaves and fishes or knew someone who had been healed. But Jesus demonstrated what he thought of his Father by what he did. As the philosopher John Locke said *"I have always thought the actions of men the best interpreters of their thoughts."* This is why the cross has such a great impact on us. The full extent of Jesus' trust in the Father shows us the full extent of their love for one another.

The Outer Garden

Totally yielded and trusting in His Father's will, Jesus is brought to the place of crucifixion. The disciples had still not made that journey of understanding why Jesus had to die. Jesus is settled in His Father's will whereas the disciples are bewildered and afraid.

Loving you is easy – Loving me is hard!

I love the story in Matthew 14 where Jesus, having heard of the execution of his cousin John, went off to a *'solitary place'* and a crowd turned up, closely followed by the disciples. Isn't that just how it is when we want to spend time alone, the door bell, the neighbour, the phone? The disciples produce a few fish and loaves and Jesus *'looking up to heaven..gave thanks...'* and the disciples proceed to hand the food out to 5000 people. After everyone had eaten their fill, the disciples start collecting all the leftovers and as they did so, I found myself asking why, on a hot, dusty day, are they collecting food from people who could take it away with them? What are they going to do with twelve baskets of leftovers when they won't be able to get themselves and all those baskets in the boat for the return journey? In my imagination I found myself saying to Jesus, *"Lord, I'm fed up of tidying up someone else's mess!"* to which He said *"Well come and sit beside me and we can watch them because I never asked them to do it anyway!"*

Whilst that was my own imagining - and I know in Johns' gospel he does ask them to collect the leftovers - God nevertheless spoke to me clearly about the fact that I often run around working for Him and doing things that He has not asked me to do. It dawned on me that the real work done that afternoon was when Jesus *'looking up to heaven'* yielded the situation to His Father and trusted Him for the outcome. This real interface of yielding and trusting between Jesus and his Father reaches its culmination at the crucifixion.

The power of yielding

The more I consider the crucifixion of Jesus, the more I understand the relationship between trust and suffering, both in the world and in my own life. The real measure of my trust in God is reflected in my willingness to yield those things that keep me stuck outside the garden.

The only way that Jesus could get into the inner garden was to yield everything. Let's think about what He had already yielded and how His trust in the Father was rewarded.

He had yielded His reputation - He was mocked by the religious men who thought they 'knew' God, but they missed His joy when lepers were healed and Lazarus was raised from the dead.

He yielded His career - there didn't seem to be too much of a future for a Messiah if the Pharisees could get their hands on him, but Nicodemus understood and his hands helped prepare Jesus body for burial! (Jn 19).
He yielded His friends and family.
His anxieties were given to the Father - "Father not my will but Yours...".
His anger, distress (Mark 3:5), the list goes on - just like ours.

As Jesus publically yielded in trust to his Father, in the crowd there were those, like Nicodemus and the Centurion, who really started to see Jesus for who He was. On the cross Jesus made a final demonstration of His trust in His Father when He yielded His spirit. What is a great comfort to me is that He did so with a loud triumphant cry "It is finished". I don't know about you but there are times I don't understand why God is asking me to yield something and I only give up with a loud cry!

It is sometimes very hard to trust God, even when we really want to, because there is a sneaking suspicion that it is going to cost us. As C S Lewis said, "*We are not necessarily doubting that God will do the best for us, we are wondering how painful the best will turn out to be.*" I also find it hard to yield something when I do understand why God is asking me to do it. I find it is a bit like the story of the vine which Jesus said gets pruned in order that it might grow and gets pruned of the bits that are dead - either way we get pruned! At least it is so that we can '*bear fruit*'!

I'm sure many of you will agree that the hardest areas to yield are those which have caused us deep pain. I mean the kind of pain that has pierced our souls and from which we feel we could barely recover - especially so when the recovery is determined by our forgiving the one/s who had done the piercing! The answer lies in how desperately do we want to enter the inner garden?

Remember the monkey and the coconut story. You may be aware of something that you are gripping in your hand and don't want to let go. It might be a relationship, possessions, attitudes or unforgiveness. It is keeping you stuck outside the gate to the inner garden and you know God is asking you to yield it and you are struggling with yourself and with God.

However here is the good news. When Jesus was dead, he was carried into the garden - isn't that an incredibly powerful picture? He had died totally to self and without doing anything Himself, He was carried into that inner garden.

Is there something you need to let die? Why not yield it now and let the Father carry you into the inner garden.

The Inner Garden

"... and in the garden a new tomb, in which no-one had ever been laid." John 19:42

The first thing Jesus received in the garden was a place of rest especially prepared for Him. Everything He needed, which He obviously couldn't do for Himself, was taken care of, His battered body cleaned and dressed in spices and fresh linen. He was treated with tenderness, dignity and respect. The tomb was a place of shelter from all that was happening outside - bitter bickering and accusations between politicians and religious leaders, shock and shame among the dispersed crowds. Imagine also if you will, the crowd leaving the scene of the crucifixion as the earth was shaking, rocks splitting, running to their homes for shelter and meeting dead people risen from their tombs who were now alive and walking amongst them! All this arose from Jesus yielding.

Meanwhile Jesus had moved from a place of total trust to a place of total rest and He hadn't had to do anything to get there except to let go and trust His Father! What happens next in this garden of rewarded trust is so awesome. On that first Easter morning there is an earthquake, the stone rolls back and an angel sits on it watching the guards shaking and passing out. The women who came to the tomb had been really scared by this impressive angel, *"His appearance was like lightening"*, but when he tells them Jesus is alive they completely lose interest in him and rush off to find Jesus. But, wonder of wonders, Jesus meets them!

And this Jesus is the same yet not the same. He is fully restored yet more than He was as a man. He ate fish with his friends yet He doesn't need food, He walked along a road to Emmaus but there is no mention of His walking back! He disappeared! They could touch His hands and feet but His body could never be damaged again. His relationship with His Father, separated for that time on the cross by our sin, was gloriously and eternally restored. And for His followers, who had great difficulty understanding some of the things He said, *"He opened their minds so they* could understand..." Luke 24:45 Their spiritual understanding was at last awakening and they were beginning that wonderful journey of discovering the full meaning of God's plan of salvation for the souls of mankind.

"We are not human beings having a spiritual experience, we are spiritual beings having a human experience." Pierre Teilhard de Chardin

Is this not a wonderful inner garden to enter? We find rest from our striving, restoration of peace in our relationship with our Creator, healing of wounds and hurts, and time to fellowship with God in a deeper and more intimate way. We are assured of His victory, the gospel will flourish and His purposes will stand.

In this garden space we don't have to do anything except allow the Holy Spirit carry us to meet with God. As Christians we want to walk in resurrection power and that power flows from anyone learning to yield, trust and rest in God.

The beautiful thing about being in the garden is that we are so engrossed in intimacy with God that, like the women who lost interest in the angel, we aren't side-tracked when all the miracles start happening around us! We learn to give time for God to speak to us or to share silence together just listening to the sound of peace.

Here is a great thought – *'garden time'* with God doesn't have to be somewhere up a mountain in the mist (with oilskins and waterproofs!), or in a place of total silence. We carry *'garden space'* in our hearts and that is available for us to enter into anytime, anywhere. We stay physically in the place we are in - the cinema, room full of people, at work - but in our heads and hearts, we can go sit down on a garden seat right next to our heavenly Father and ask a question, wait for Him to say something or, just enjoying watching the garden together. It's the inner place of transformational power.

Reflective Exercises

1 Think of what your garden would look like. Imagine God is waiting for you to enter the garden where He is. Is there anything that would hold you back from entering the garden? Is there anything you would like to let go of so that you can meet with the Lord? It might be that you just need to open the gate and trust everything will be fine.

2 Our 'garden' is in our hearts and minds. Take a moment at any point during the day and go through the 'gate' into God's presence. Bring what is on your mind to the Lord and leave it with Him. How does it feel to leave things in God's Hands? It may be that your heart is filled with thankfulness at knowing God has listened and spoken to you.

3 Think of Bible verses or passages that speak to you of God's unconditional love. You might like to write a few of them in your journal. Take one of the verses with you into the garden with God. What might you like to say to Him about what this verse means to you? Reflect on what the Lord might be saying to you through this verse.

4 Look back on your life. You may recall great times and very hard times. As you think of the garden that was prepared for Jesus when He was crucified, can you see where God has put a garden that had a gift from Him to you in your good and hard times? It may be He provided someone who 'just happened' to be there, or financial help or a timely conversation. You might like to journal your thoughts as an encouragement for the future.

Bible verses worth exploring

1 Psalm 37:3, 4   It's interesting to think about why delighting in the Lord goes hand in hand with receiving the desires of our heart.

2 Song of Songs 6:2   Here is a picture of someone not just walking in a garden but 'browsing' and 'gathering'.   It speaks of reflection and appreciation and purpose. It is good to take time to listen to the birds and to smell the flowers.   Perhaps learning to slow down is something that would be of benefit for you.

3 Deuteronomy 33:12 This image of resting between the Lord's shoulders is a bit like a child having a 'piggyback' ride from their father. Is there something in this image that opens up aspects of God as your Father? It might make you smile, or want to laugh, or just settle down for a journey where God is going to take you places and show you special things. You might like to journal where the journey takes you!

4 John 7:37 Can you hear the passion in Jesus' voice asking the thirsty to come to Him? Is there someone you might like to bring to Jesus so that they can have their thirst satisfied on the inside?

For Reflection

A Modern version of the 23rd Psalm

The Lord is my Pacesetter – I shall not rush.
He makes me stop for quiet intervals,
He provides me with images of stillness which restore my serenity,
He leads me in ways of efficiency through calmness of mind,
And His guidance is peace.
Even though I have a great many things to
accomplish each day, I will not fret,
For His Presence is here,
His timelessness, His all importance, will keep
me in balance.
He prepares refreshment and renewal in the midst of my activity,
By anointing my mind with His oils of tranquility,
My cup of joyous energy overflows.
Truly harmony and effectiveness shall be
the fruits of my hours,
For I shall walk in the Pace of my Lord
And dwell in His House for ever.

By a Japanese writer – Tokio Megashie

Chapter 6 The Butterfly Women

One of my favourite things to do is to sit in the garden and watch quietly as birds come to the birdbath and all sorts of wildlife enter the garden – in between all the rain we have in Scotland! Seeing butterflies come to the flowers is particularly sweet and I love watching how they dance together, then separate to go to other bushes and then come back again. It is incredible that butterflies can travel thousands of miles – the Monarch butterfly from the Eastern United States flies to Mexico using the sun to help them find their way.

"We delight in the beauty of the butterfly, but rarely admit the changes it has gone through to achieve that beauty". Author unknown.

For a butterfly to become a butterfly, a transformation has to take place. After the chrysalis stage, the butterfly needs *'breakthrough'* to take flight as a fully formed adult. Breakthrough is one of the key themes that takes placein the gardens of God. This leads me on to a dream I had some years ago and it is something I'd like to share with you. Take what is relevant and a blessing to you and, bin what isn't!

<u>The Dream</u>

One night some years ago, I had a very vivid spiritual dream. I was sitting on an airplane at a table – similar to tables on trains - facing the direction of travel, with my hands resting on the table. Opposite me sat a smartly dressed man and across the aisle on my right were two more men, speaking what sounded like Dutch. As I looked out of the airplane, I was aware of large objects flying past the window - ship containers, lorries and packing cases of all sizes! I began to feel anxious about how the plane was going to get to its destination, when the man opposite me reached across, stroked one of my fingers and said, *"Don't worry we will get there safely"*. I fell into a deep sleep.

When I awoke the plane had landed and I started to walk towards the front exit of the plane. There were no seats or other passengers - just a spacious area. As I walked forward, the exit door opened and two men came in, carrying a painting on an easel, which they put down in front of me. The painting was of a wide blue river with ripe wheat fields on either side. The sky was blue, the sun was shining and on the river was a wide canoe-shaped boat, sitting across the breadth of the river. In the boat were 10 or so woman sitting with their backs to me, all wearing the same long, light brown, elegant dresses. On their heads were medieval style hats shaped like butterflies.

Suddenly, the painting came to life: the river sparkled, the ripe wheat swayed in the warm breeze and the warmth of the sun was wonderful. As I watched, the women in the boat all started to laugh with great joy, picked up fishing rods and cast out into the river. They were filled with joy and rejoiced with each other as they caught large fish which they brought into the boat. One of the men said to me, "*What could you do with that?*" to which I replied, "*What could I do with that...?!.*" when I was filled with ecstatic joy and woke up!

I began to explore the dream. Who were these '*butterfly*' women, why were their hats shaped like butterflies and what was the meaning of them laughing and pulling fish into the boat?

I happened to be reading in the Book of Judges Chapter 4 and 4, about Deborah, (her name means 'Bee') and thought about how butterflies pollinate and bring fruitfulness. In the book of Judges, Deborah was bringing advice and leadership to a nation when she sends for Barak to ask him to lead the nation in battle against oppressors. Barak* is very nervous about this. Actually, if I'd been minding my own business when, out of the blue, someone comes and tells me I have to lead a battle, I'd have been very reluctant myself! In the end, Barak goes with Deborah and the promised victory is achieved – through another woman, Jael, who goes with her husband when he decides to upsticks and leave the rest of his tribe to pitch his tent under some trees in the '*wilderness*' - for no apparent reason!

But, look at the Song of Deborah and Barak after the battle – amazing words which I leave you to explore.

I have met many '*butterfly women*' over the years and wanted to share some thoughts to encourage you in whatever situation you may find yourself. You may find it helpful to have a Bible to hand! I believe that the '*butterfly women*' are women who, like Deborah (Book of Judges), Esther (Book of Esther), Jael (Judges), Lydia (Book of Acts) and many more, through everything, have chosen to keep following the Lord even though at times they may have felt abandoned, distressed, anonymous or taken to the wire. This doesn't mean there haven't also been times of great blessing. Their strength is in the Lord for He has become their sufficiency and satisfaction. Their desire is to follow Christ and bring people to faith in Him. They live that passion practically through every area of their lives. It has the effect of restoring and encouraging men into headship and leadership. Most importantly, they are willing to step up to the mark when the Lord calls.

You might be feeling like Jael, whose husband Heber the Kenite left the rest of the Kenites and pitched his tent near some trees in what seemed like the wilderness (Judges), yet when Sisera comes past, Jael is in the right place at the right time to deal with him. Crucially, she stepped up to the mark when the Lord needed her to. The same is true of Esther – she was in the right place at the right time but could have been overwhelmed with fear and fled rather than step up to the mark to save her people.

In these days of upheaval, we are told in Isaiah 8:12,13 *"Do not call conspiracy everything that these people call conspiracy; do not fear what they fear, and do not dread it. The Lord Almighty is the one you are to regard as holy."*

You may not feel like a Deborah but the Lord knows your life's story and circumstances. All you have to do is trust Him, enjoy whatever and wherever the adventure takes you and be ready – for you will bring fruitfulness and blessing to all those whose lives you touch.

May you follow Him with all your hearts, pursue peace and sanctuary garden space, keep oil in your lamps and step up to the mark to stand in the gates with joy and awesome faith in Him.

'He will be a spirit of justice to those who sit in judgement and a source of strength to those who turn back the battle at the gates' Isaiah 28:6

*In Rabbinical literature Barak was a humble man who, unsure of how he could be of particular service to God, took his wife's suggestion to make offering candles for the sanctuary of Shiloh. Deborah, therefore, is known as "the wife of Lappidoth" - Torchlights! The Lord said to them that because of their humble desire to make large candles to light up the sanctuary, He would make the light of their lives shine brightly.

References:

23rd Psalm version, http://www.appleseeds.org/Ps-23_Explained.htm

Dr Frank Lake (1914 – 1982), Clinical Theologian,
http://www.bridgepastoral.org.uk/history/frankLake.htm

Erik Erikson , Stages of Psychosocial Development,
http://psychology.about.com/library/bl_psychosocial_summary.htm

Eric Berne (1910 - 1970), Transactional analysis in Psychotherapy,
http://www.ericberne.com/transactional-analysis/

Mother Theresa of Calcutta (1910-1997),
http://prayerfoundation.org/mother_teresa_do_it_anyway.htm

Tokio Megashie Japanese 23rd psalm,
http://re-worship.blogspot.co.uk/2011/05/psalm-23-lord-is-my-pace-setter.html

David Johnson and Jeff Vanvonderen: *'The Subtle Power of Spiritual Abuse'*

M Scott Peck: *'People of the Lie'*

35147700R00045

Made in the USA
Charleston, SC
29 October 2014